THEMES for early years PHOTOCOPIABLES

FESTIVALS

EDITOR

Sally Gray

ASSISTANT EDITOR

Lesley Sudlow

ILLUSTRATOR

Kate Davies

COVER

Lynne Joesbury

SERIES DESIGNER

Sarah Rock

DESIGNER

Anna Oliwa

AUTHOR

Pauline Kenyon

Published by Scholastic Ltd,
Villiers House, Clarendon Avenue,
Leamington Spa, Warwickshire CV32 5PR

British Library Cataloguing-in-Publication Data
A catalogue record for this book is available from the British Library.

ISBN 0-439-01695-9

CONTENTS

AUTUMN FESTIVALS

WINTER FESTIVALS

INTRODUCTION

Using themes

The *Themes for Early Years Photocopiables* series is designed to supplement and build on the existing *Themes for Early Years* series. *Festivals* is divided into four chapters covering spring, summer, autumn and winter festivals. The range of photocopiable sheets and activities have been carefully chosen to complement and build on two existing titles *Themes for Early Years – Spring and Summer Festivals* and *Themes for Early Years – Autumn and Winter Festivals*.

The book is intended to support all those who work in playgroups, voluntary groups, nurseries and reception classes. The activities provide a valuable bank of children's tasks which follow a year's cycle of festivals, special days and celebrations from many backgrounds and the world's major faiths. The chapters follow the seasons and are set out in chronological order for ease of planning and use over an annual cycle to provide a year's worth (or more) of multi-faith and multicultural work.

How to use this book

The ideas in the book will help busy early years providers in their planning and provision of activities across the six Areas of Learning prescribed by the QCA's Early Learning Goals. By the nature of the 'festivals' theme, all the activities apply to the Personal, social and emotional development area, with the children finding out about people from other cultures. For this reason no specific activities have been ascribed to this area, as all fall within this remit. Many of the activities are linked to the area of Knowledge and understanding, covering aspects of technology, history, geography, religious education and science.

Most of the suggested activities actually cover several Areas of Learning but only the predominant learning objective is highlighted. The vast majority will involve children in personal and social interaction and the development of fine motor skills linked to physical development requirements.

The book is divided into four chapters with 'spring' covering the months March to May, 'summer' covering June to August, 'autumn' covering September to November and 'winter' covering December to February.

Each of the four chapters begins with four pages of teachers' notes that act as a guide to the following photocopiable activity sheets. The activities are designed to be linked to play and to provide active and enjoyable tasks. Information on the specific festivals featured is included on pages 7 to 10.

The activities are aimed at children aged three-to-five years, working in different-sized groups to suit the task. Each photocopiable activity sheet has a clear learning objective identified and teachers' notes give guidance on how to lead the activity successfully to achieve this target. Suggested questions to ask the group and useful vocabulary to emphasize

are included. Some activities also include ideas for supporting younger, or extending older children's learning, where appropriate.

The teachers' notes for each activity, plus the relevant festival background information, could be photocopied, mounted on card and then used to support volunteers and parents who are helping with particular groups. A bank of these 'Helpers' cards' could be developed – saving busy staff time when organizing their different activities.

The completed photocopiable sheets can also form a useful record of the children's work and can be dated and kept for assessment.

Festivals

Background information on the different festivals and their religious significance is included in this book to help staff feel confident in setting the context of any work. It will be useful to read the festival background and introduce the children to the idea of each festival before embarking on the activities, so that staff can remind children of the main features of each special day or celebration and reinforce their learning as they enjoy the related tasks. Wherever possible, it will be beneficial to collect a range of pictures, books and artefacts for children to refer to.

Many settings will already plan to celebrate a range of major festivals, and you will find that most of the activities will result in children's work that can be used for colourful displays, enhancing festival celebrations in the nursery. You may also find a selection of intriguing and exciting festivals that are new to you which will bring a new dimension to your nursery year!

The activities in this book are set out in chronological order, however, you can choose to begin the cycle wherever you wish. In this way, it is possible to plan to cover specific festivals over a year.

Although the dates of the festivals are currently correct, remember that some festivals, such as Eid-ul-Fitr and Easter, are moveable feasts with dates that vary from year to year.

Many of the festivals commonly celebrated in early years, such as Harvest, Divali, Christmas and Eid-ul-Fitr, have more than one activity. This should help to provide valuable resources for use in settings with more than one age group, so that activities are not repeated as children progress through the nursery.

Home links

Some activities also lend themselves to involving parents and the community, such as those concerned with making Eid and Divali cards, a letter to Father Christmas and Mother's Day gift containers. It will be useful for you to look for local links to develop the children's learning, for instance with a visit to a Gurdwara or synagogue, or to arrange a visit from a parent to talk about their family celebrations.

FESTIVALS

Spring

St David's Day (1 March)

St David is the patron saint of Wales. His symbols of the daffodil or the leek are worn on his special day.

Holi (1 March)

A Hindu festival of love which celebrates God's protection for true believers. It remembers Prahlada who refused to worship a king, whatever punishment he ordered.

Mother's Day (March)

Originally called Mothering Sunday, this was a holiday for young girls working in service away from home. They could use the day to visit their mothers and give gifts.

Easter (March/April)

An important Christian festival to mark the joy of Jesus' resurrection after the misery of his crucifixion on Good Friday. The egg, a symbol of new life and hope, has become associated with Easter. People exchange chocolate eggs, cards and decorate real eggs. The actual name 'Easter' comes from the Saxon goddess 'Eastre', who brought the spring each year.

St Patrick's Day (17 March)

St Patrick was captured by pirates as a young man but escaped to settle in Ireland. He became a renowned leader and patron saint of Ireland.

Pesach (April)

Pesach is the Jewish festival of Passover. It commemorates the hardships of the Israelites who Moses led out of slavery in Egypt, towards the 'Promised Land'. At this time, Jews remember the ten plagues sent by God to gain their freedom from the Pharaoh. In particular, they remember the Passover night when the first born in every family died, except in those Israelite houses which had been specially marked. It was this that convinced the Pharaoh to let the slaves leave with Moses.

Purim (Four weeks before Pesach)

This lively festival celebrates the time when Queen Esther outwitted Haman, when she discovered that he planned to kill the Persian Jews. The story is read in the synagogue and everyone makes loud noises so that Haman's name cannot be heard.

All Fool's Day (1 April)

A day when people play tricks on each other – but only until 12 noon. In France, people give each other 'April fishes' (usually made of chocolate). This may stem from the sixteenth century when the French date of New Year changed from 1 April to 1 January.

Baisakhi (13 April)

The Sikh New Year is one of the most important Sikh celebrations. It remembers the five volunteers who were ready to sacrifice themselves at Guru Gobind Singh's request. They became the first Khalsa. Since then, baptised Sikhs wear the 'five K's': the kirpan (sword) to defend the good and poor; the kara (bracelet) to remember God's love; kesh – a command never to cut their hair; a kangha (comb) and kachera (shorts).

St George's Day (23 April)

St George is the patron saint of England who is supposed to have slain a horrific dragon that was devouring humans. He may be based on a Christian Roman soldier who led a righteous life fighting evil. His flag is a red cross on a white background and his symbol is a rose. Shakespeare's birthday is also celebrated on 23 April.

May Day (1 May)

The traditions of May Day go back to Roman and Celtic times, celebrating the goddess Flora (associated with flowers). There are local customs of processions, greeting the dawn, dancing and selecting a May Queen.

Children's Day (5 May)

A Japanese festival (formerly Boys' Day) with celebrations linked to strength and perseverance. The symbols are carp – full of energy and power – and irises, to represent the swords of Samurai warriors. Celebrations include feasting and drinking to build up strength!

Summer

Shavuot (May)

Sometimes called the Festival of Weeks, this festival is held seven weeks after Pesach. It celebrates a story from the Torah, when God gave Moses the ten commandments. At Shavuot, synagogues are decorated with dairy foods, fruit and flowers. At home, Jews eat a special bread with a ladder pattern on it, to remind them that Moses climbed the mountain.

Dragon Boat Festival (June)

This Chinese festival is a reminder of the bravery of a wise leader, Ch'u Yuan, who threw himself into a lake rather than carry out the Emperor's orders to tax the starving people. To protect his body from evil monsters, the local people threw lumps of rice into the water and raced out to retrieve his body. The Dragon Boat race celebrates this story. People eat rice dumplings and salted duck eggs at this time.

Wesak (May/June)

This Theravada Buddhist festival celebrates the three major events of Buddha's life – his birth, his enlightenment and his death – all of which happened on the same date in different years.

People give gifts to the poor and decorate their homes and temples with flowers, lanterns, candles and incense. It is not a feast day, so no special food is eaten.

Raksha Bandhan (July or August)

This Hindu festival originates from a story about the God Indra. His wife tied a special thread around his wrist and it saved him from an evil demon. Today, people think about caring for their families – especially brothers and sisters. Girls tie a rakhi round their brothers' wrist to protect him and give him strength to protect her.

Father's Day (June)

A modern festival when children give love and thanks to their fathers.

Midsummer's Day (24 June)

A festival associated with Druids. It falls on the longest day of sunlight and ceremonies are held at places where the sun is particularly visible, such as Stonehenge. Some people believe that it is a special day for marriage and naming ceremonies.

St Swithin's Day (15 July)

Legend has it that, if it rains on St Swithin's Day, it will continue to rain for 40 days and 40 nights.

O'bon (Mid-July)

This is the most important Buddhist festival in Japan. It is a time when families remember their relatives who have died. They believe that their dead relatives' spirits return to the family home for the three days of the festival. They light lamps to show them the way home and put flowers on the family shrine. Special fires are lit to make the arrival and departure of the spirits a joyful occasion.

Ganesh-Chaturthi (28 August)

This Hindu festival celebrates the birthday of Ganesha, the elephant-headed god. Hindu stories say that Ganesha is Shiva's son, and that one day when Shiva was in a temper, he cut off Ganesha's head and gave him an elephant's head in its place.

Ganesha is seen as the remover of all obstacles and difficulties and he is traditionally worshipped at the beginning of all new projects or endeavours, such as marriages and when people move house.

Autumn

Chinese Moon Festival (September)

This occurs in September, the eighth lunar month when the moon is at its brightest. It is also called the Mid-Autumn or Lantern Festival. It recalls the story of the evil Chinese king who obtained a potion which would make him live for ever. His wife Sheung Ngao dreaded her husband making the people suffer forever, so she drank the potion herself. The king tried to kill her but the gods transported her to the moon to live forever and shine kindly on her people. Today, people make colourful lanterns, often of fish and animals for the festival, which are lit as darkness falls. People eat 'moon cakes' (pastry cases filled with lotus or melon). It is a popular time for family gatherings as well as weddings and engagements.

Ethiopian New Year (11 September)

Rastafarians celebrate their new year with family and community celebrations. Drumming is an important part of the event, as they remember their African heritage, particularly in Ethiopia.

Sukkot (September/October)

This Jewish festival, also known as the Feast of the Tabernacles, lasts for a week. It celebrates harvest and commemorates the time when the Israelites were protected by God as they wandered in the wilderness. Many Jewish families build a 'sukkah', or hut, in their gardens and live in it for the week to remind them of how their ancestors lived in temporary shelters. At the synagogue, people process carrying the 'lulav' (the palm branch), the 'hadas' (myrtle) and the 'ravah' (willow) in their left hand and an etrog (citrus fruit) in their right. The Torah is carried around. At the end of Sukkot, children are given sweets and fruit.

Harvest (September/October)

Around the world, at harvest, people gather to give thanks for the fruits of the earth. Local communities traditionally gather for a Harvest Supper, to celebrate once the crops are all safely gathered in. The giving of food to the poor is an important feature of world-wide harvest celebrations.

Grandparent's Day (September)

A new festival in which children and families thank their grandparents. Cards and gifts may be given and family reunions held.

Divali (October/November)

Hindus and Sikhs celebrate this festival and decorate their homes with divas (small oil lamps). Hindus recall the story of Rama and Sita and their fourteen year banishment from their kingdom, emphasizing the eventual triumph of goodness over evil.

Sikhs recall the story of the sixth Guru, Guru Hargobind, who was imprisoned by the Mogul Emperor, along with 52 Sikh princes. The Emperor agreed to let Hargobind go, plus any others who could leave by a narrow passage still holding the Guru's cloak. The Guru had a special cloak made with long tapes and led all the princes to safety.

Bonfire Night (5 November)

This British celebration commemorates the unsuccessful attempt to blow up the Houses of Parliament in 1605. Guy Fawkes and many of the others who plotted to destroy the king were found and later executed. The Yeomen of the Guard still search the vaults each year on this date before Parliament is opened.

Guru Nanak's Birthday (25 November)

This Sikh festival is celebrated in November, although Guru Nanak was born in April. Guru Nanak started the Sikh faith from his belief that all people should work together and worship one god. He travelled to teach Sikhs and share his wisdom. He was concerned for the welfare of the poor, introducing the idea of the 'langar' (free kitchen).

St Andrew's Day (30 November)

St Andrew is the patron saint of Scotland. He was one of Jesus' disciples. His flag is a white diagonal cross on a blue background.

Winter

Hanukkah (December)

This Jewish festival of light lasts for eight days. It commemorates Judah defeating the Syrians and reclaiming their Temple in Jerusalem. The Syrians had let the Temple menorah go out. There was only oil for one night and it would take eight days to get more. The light miraculously continued to burn until new supplies arrived. Today, Jewish families light one more candle in the hanukiah (nine-pronged candlestick) each night, until all are lit.

Advent (December)

This is the Christian period of preparation for Christ's birth. It begins on the fourth Sunday before Christmas and ends on Christmas Day. Each Sunday in churches and some homes a candle is lit on an Advent crown until all four are alight for Christmas. Children have Advent calendars and open a numbered window each day during this period.

Christmas Day (25 December)

All over the world, Christians celebrate the birth of Christ. People decorate their homes, exchange gifts and cards and eat a special dinner. In most countries, children receive a visit from Father Christmas.

New Year's Day (1 January)

Most countries greet the New Year with parties and celebrations. In Scotland Hogmanay is celebrated with Scottish dancing, fun and feasting.

Epiphany (6 January)

This Christian church festival commemorates the arrival of the wise men to see baby Jesus and to bring him gifts of gold, frankincense and myrrh. Traditionally it marks the end of Christmas celebrations and is the date when decorations are taken down and packed away.

Chinese New Year (January/February)

An important Chinese festival that lasts for fifteen days. The exact date depends on the new moon. Each year is named after one of the twelve animals who raced to settle an argument. The years are named in the order the animals finished the race: rat, ox, tiger, hare, dragon, snake, horse, ram, monkey, cockerel, dog and pig.

Eid-ul-Fitr

This Muslim festival is held at the end of Ramadan, the month when Muslims fast between sunrise and sunset. The date varies depending on the appearance of the new moon. Before the festival begins, Muslims give money to the poor. The festival commences with a celebratory meal before going to the mosque to give thanks and pray.

Candlemas (2 February)

This Christian festival commemorates Mary presenting Jesus to the Temple, as required by Jewish law. At special church services, children are often presented with a candle.

Pancake Day (February/March)

This is the Christian festival of Shrove Tuesday and is the day before Ash Wednesday and the beginning of Lent. Traditionally, Christians fasted during Lent as a reminder of Jesus fasting in the wilderness. Pancakes were prepared on Shrove Tuesday to use up some of the foodstuffs that could not be eaten during the Lent period.

Mardi Gras

This literally means 'Greasy or Fat Tuesday' and is the same festival as Shrove Tuesday. Many countries celebrate Mardi Gras with processions and Carnivals.

Valentine's Day (14 February)

On this day, people traditionally send unsigned cards to those they secretly love. Legend has it that it is the date that birds choose their mates and begin to build nests. Valentine himself was probably Bishop Valentine, a third-century Roman soldier who refused to agree to the command that soldiers must not marry but devote themselves to their fighting careers. He was imprisoned, and finally executed on 14 February.

SPRING FESTIVALS

PAGE 15
ST DAVID'S DAY – DAFFODILS

Learning objectives
To understand how numbers of objects can be added together and to begin to use mathematical language. (Mathematics)

Group size
Four to six children.

Show the children some daffodils (real or silk). Talk about daffodils growing wild or in gardens. If the flowers are real, let the children touch and smell them. Divide the flowers into two small groups and say: 'I have three flowers here and two more there, let's see how many we have altogether?'. Count each flower together saying: 'Three add two equals five'. Repeat with different numbers. Give each child a copy of the photocopiable sheet and let them count each clump. Explain what the addition symbol means. Help younger children to count and write the numbers in the spaces.

PAGE 16
HOLI – HOLI COLOURS

Learning objective
To learn to mix colours together to make new colours. (Creative Development)

Group size
Four children.

Prepare pots of yellow, blue and red paint, palettes, water pots and small brushes. Give each child a copy of the photocopiable sheet and let them paint in the red powder pile. Show them how to hold and wash their brush correctly. Invite them to paint the yellow pile. Then ask: 'What will happen if you mix the colours?'. Let them put a little red and yellow in a palette and mix it. Can the children describe the colour they have made? Let them paint in the final pile. Repeat with the other rows. Finally, let them choose their favourite colour to complete the sheet.

PAGE 17
HOLI – ANIMAL MARCH

Learning objective
To order animals by size. (Mathematics)

Group size
Six to eight children.

Show the group a collection of different-sized animals and ask them to choose the biggest and the smallest one. Arrange them on a surface. Now ask each child in turn to pick an animal and ask them if it is bigger or smaller than the others. Place it in the middle. Repeat with each of the animals, saying: 'Is it bigger than this one?' and 'Where does it go in order of size?'. Now give each child a copy of the photocopiable sheet. Invite them to cut out the elephants and stick them on a piece of paper in order of size.

PAGE 18
MOTHER'S DAY – GIFT BOWL

Learning objectives
To explore materials and develop cutting, folding and joining skills. (Physical Development)

Group size
Four children.

Provide each child with a photocopiable sheet copied onto card and 60cm of thin ribbon. Explain that they are going to make a container, from the photocopiable sheet, as a present for their mummy. Help them to cut carefully around the shape. Use a hole punch to make the holes and let them decorate both sides of the bowl. Help them to fold the flaps towards the centre and show them how to thread the ribbon through the holes, pulling it to shape the bowl. Tie in a bow and as a finishing touch, fill with sweets or home-made biscuits.

PAGE 19

ST PATRICK'S DAY – SHAMROCK SPRIGS

Learning objective
To count and match numbers. (Mathematics)

Group size
Six children.

Provide each child with a copy of the photocopiable sheet and a green felt-tipped pen. Explain that the shamrock is the emblem of Ireland and that many Irish people wear a bunch to commemorate St Patrick's Day. If possible, show the children a piece of shamrock or a clover leaf. Before looking at the pictures and number labels on the sheet, explain to the children that some of the shamrock is missing. Ask them to count each sprig and to draw some more shamrocks to match the label. Show them how to use the number line to help.

PAGE 20

EASTER – THE EASTER STORY

Learning objective
To sequence the events of the Easter story. (Language and Literacy)

Group size
Eight children.

Tell the children a simple version of the Easter story. Ask them to imagine how the different people in the story would have felt. Give each child a copy of the photocopiable sheet and recap the story with them. Let the children cut out the pictures and encourage them to arrange the pictures in the order of the story. Invite them to retell the story to you, using the pictures to help them.

PAGE 21

EASTER – CHICKEN AND EGG

Learning objective
To learn about a simple life cycle. (Knowledge and Understanding of the World)

Group size
Six children.

Explain to the children that when a hen lays her eggs, she keeps them nice and warm until they are ready to hatch. Talk about and describe the wonderful moment when the tiny chick struggles out of the shell, and then later becomes an adult hen.

Give each child a copy of the photocopiable sheet and help them to write a caption under each picture, acting as scribe for younger children. Ask them to cut them out and arrange them in a cycle. Talk about how the cycle goes on and on, unless it's broken. Can the children suggest how the cycle might be broken?

PAGE 22

PESACH – PESACH SEDER

Give each child a copy of the photocopiable sheet and look at it together. What foods do they recognize? Tell them what the unusual foods are and explain that these are for the special Seder celebration. Tell the children that the foods are not eaten but they all have special meanings to the Jewish people. Ask the children to tell you about any special family celebration meals they can remember. What foods did they share? How were these special? Ask the children to cut out the foods and carefully match and stick them to the dish. Read the names to the children and practise saying them out loud.

Learning objective
To learn about the special food for the Passover feast. (Knowledge and Understanding of the World)

Group size
Four to six children.

PAGE 23

PESACH – DAVID'S STAR

Provide each child with a copy of the photocopiable sheet, mounted onto thin card. Show the children the star on the Seder plate (page 22) and explain that this is a special Jewish symbol which often decorates Jewish things. Ask them about any other symbols they know (such as logos, crests, crosses and so on). Let the children cut out the triangle shapes. Help younger children to cut out the middles and the apex slit. Use the Seder plate design as a pattern and help them weave the triangles under and over to make the star. Close the stars with sticky tape and suspend them.

Learning objective
To make a Star of David symbol. (Physical Development)

Group size
Three or four children.

PAGE 24

PURIM – HOW MANY HATS?

Learning objective
To match Haman's hats with figures. (Mathematics)

Group size
Six to eight children.

Talk about foods which resemble other things such as gingerbread folk, shaped birthday cakes and Easter eggs. Explain that Jewish children have Hamantashen (sweet pastries, shaped like hats or purses of long ago) to celebrate Purim. Provide a number line and give each child a copy of the photocopiable sheet. Count the 'hats' together and show them how to complete the sentence with a number. Let them repeat this for each one. Help the youngest children with numeral formation or act as scribe.

PAGE 25

ALL FOOL'S DAY – FRENCH FISH

Learning objectives
To complete patterns and make a *poisson d'avril*. (Creative Development)

Group size
Four children.

Talk about April Fool's Day and how French people give each other 'April Fishes' as a joke. Give each child a copy of the photocopiable sheet and ask the children to say what parts of the fish are missing. Ask them how they can make each fish look the same. Count the scales and the stripes on the fish together. Let the children complete the patterns, colour the fish and cut them out. Help them to staple the shapes together, leaving a small gap. Ask the children to chop up the off-cuts and gently stuff the fish to make it three-dimensional. Display the fish, suspended from threads.

PAGE 26

BAISAKHI – THE KHALSA STORY

Learning objective
To sequence the story of the Khalsa. (Language and Literacy)

Group size
Three or four children.

Remind the children of the story of the five brave Sikhs. Get them to talk about what is going on in each picture, asking them to look closely at the detail (for example, the blooded sword). Ask: 'How did the people feel? When were they frightened? When were they happy?' and 'Why was the Guru a clever man?'. Then, help the children to cut out the pictures and put them in sequence. Ask them to write the numerals from 1-4 onto the right illustration and write a caption. Act as scribe for younger children.

PAGE 27

ST GEORGE'S DAY – LETTER LINKS

Learning objective
To match initial letter sounds to everyday objects. (Language and Literacy)

Group size
Eight children.

Say the word 'Saint' and emphasize the 's' sound. Let the children repeat it and play I-Spy to spot things around them beginning with 's'. Repeat with 'dragon'. Look at the photocopiable sheet together and ask the children to tell you what all the objects are. Let them join the 's' words to St George and the 'd' words to the dragon. Ask them to count who has the most. Invite older children to draw other 's' and 'd' objects. How many can they think of?

PAGE 28

MAY DAY – MAY PARADE

Learning objective
To make a May Day banner and parade with it. (Physical Development)

Group size
Four children.

Gather together some small sticks, sticky tape and scraps of bright paper and foil. Have the children ever seen a procession? Explain that people often carry banners in a procession. The banners usually have pictures that relate to the local area, or they may be linked to the month of May and springtime. Provide each child with a copy of the photocopiable sheet. What will they put on their banners? Ask

them to use their ideas to make a banner using collage materials. Fold the top edge over a stick, fastening a second stick down the back as a carrying pole. Have a May Day procession parading the completed banners.

PAGE 29
MAY DAY – SPRING FLOWERS

Learning objective
To make simple 3-D constructions. (Creative Development)

Group size
Three children.

Talk to the children about flowers growing in the spring. Show them some spring flowers and encourage them to talk about the shapes, colours and patterns that they can see. Can the children tell you which parts of the flower are the petals, stems and leaves? Give each child a copy of the photocopiable sheet and help them to cut out the flower components. Let them colour the parts appropriately. Show them how to cut, roll and fold the trumpet flaps, then help them fasten the stem and flower trumpet in place. Let older children label the different parts. Display them in sand-filled flower pots.

PAGE 30
CHILDREN'S DAY – CARP LANTERNS

Learning objective
To discriminate between long and short objects. (Mathematics)

Group size
Six to eight children.

Have a collection of long and short objects. Hold each one up and say: 'Is this long or short?'. Then compare two different objects and ask: 'Which one is longer/shorter than the other one?'. Emphasize the difference in length. Give each child a copy of the photocopiable sheet and a red and yellow coloured pencil. Look at the first picture and ask: 'Which is the longest fish lantern? Colour it red.'. Repeat for the short lantern, using yellow. Let the children complete all the other comparisons. Ask older children to decide which is the overall longest and shortest lantern.

PAGE 31
CHILDREN'S DAY – IRIS HUNT

Learning objective
To follow a route map to find the irises. (Knowledge and Understanding of the World)

Group size
Four children.

Use a dice marked 1 to 6. Provide a counter and a copy of the photocopiable sheet (enlarged if possible) for each child. Talk to the children about maps and how people find their way to new places. Explain how the photocopiable sheet is a map to help them find all the irises. Take turns with the dice and help the children to count their moves. When they land on a square, they must move in the direction of the arrow. See who can land on the most irises.

PAGE 32
CHILDREN'S DAY – HIDDEN FISH

Learning objectives
To use observation skills and to develop mathematical language. (Mathematics)

Group size
Four to six children.

Give each child a copy of the photocopiable sheet and ask them what they can see. Talk about the pond, bridge, reeds and water-lilies and animals that live in or near the water. Tell them that ten fish are hiding in the pond somewhere. Ask them to find and circle them, numbering them as they go. When all the fish are discovered, ask each child in turn: 'Tell me where your number (1) fish is hiding. Is he in the top or bottom pool? What is he next to?'.

Daffodils

◆ Add the flowers together.

2   +   3   =

4   +   2   =

3   +   5   =

1   +   2   +   3   =

Holi colours

◆ Mix the colours.

red + yellow make

blue + yellow make

red + blue make

My favourite colour is

Animal march

◆ Cut out the elephants and put them in order of size.

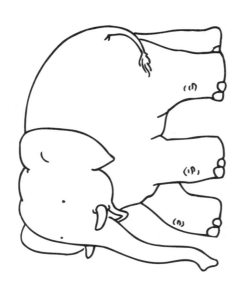

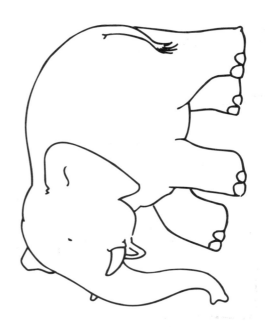

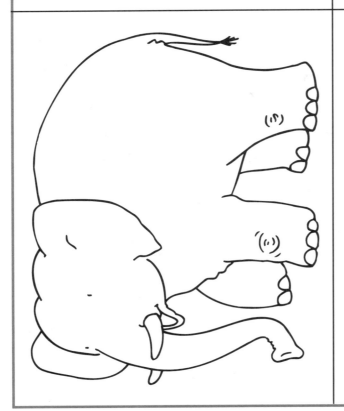

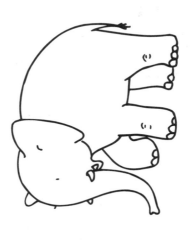

Gift bowl

◆ Cut out, fold and thread to make a bowl.

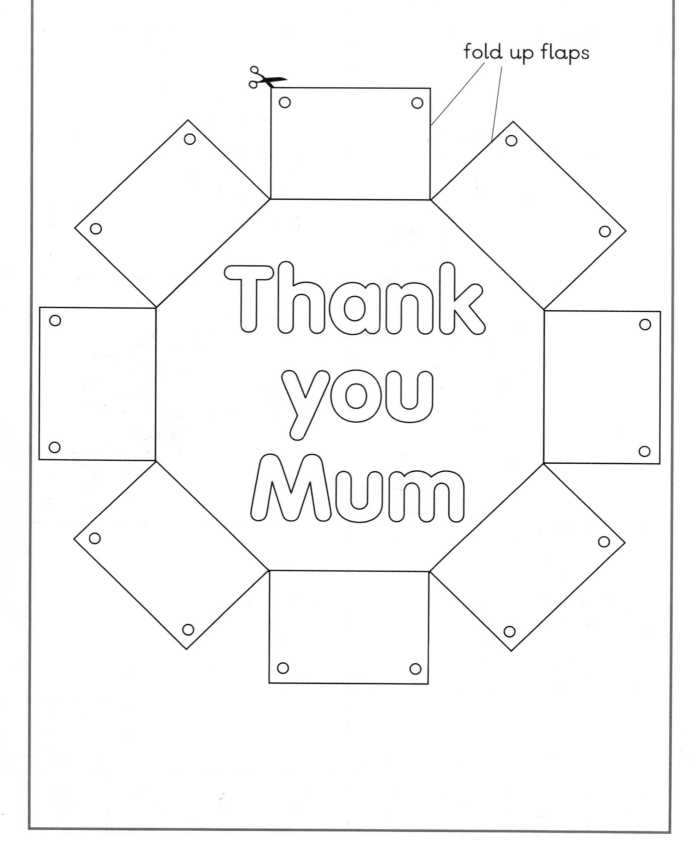

fold up flaps

Thank you Mum

Shamrock sprigs

◆ Draw the missing sprigs.

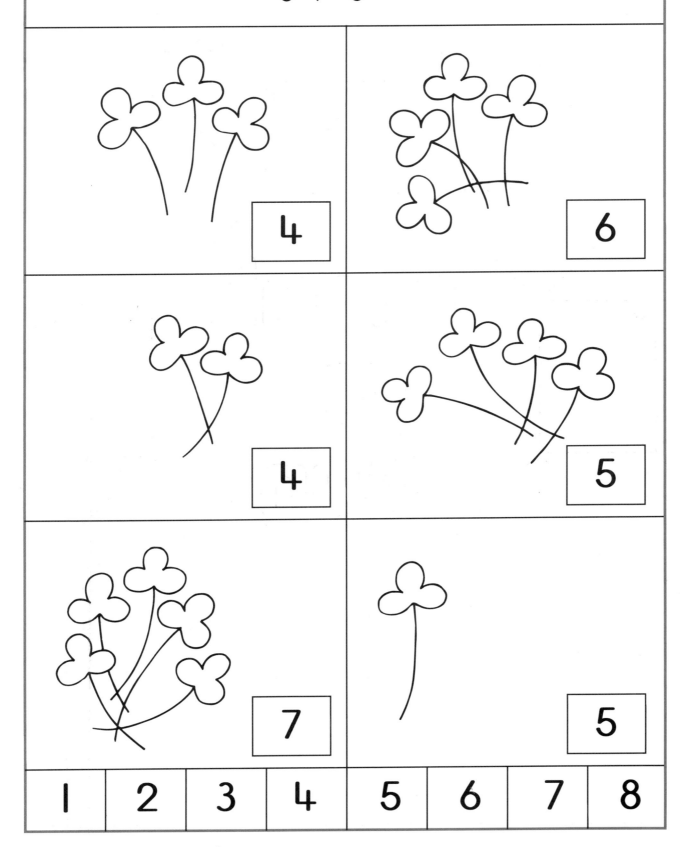

| 1 | 2 | 3 | 4 | 5 | 6 | 7 | 8 |

The Easter story

◆ Cut out the pictures and tell the story.

Chicken and egg

◆ Cut out to make a life cycle.

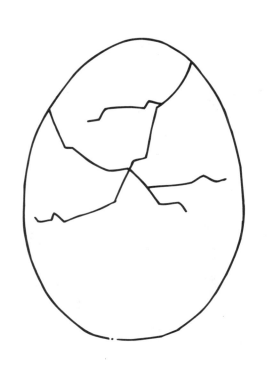

Pesach Seder

◆ Put the special foods on the Seder plate.

| egg | lamb bone | matzah |
| parsley | bitter herbs | charoset |

David's star

◆ Cut out the triangles and make a star.

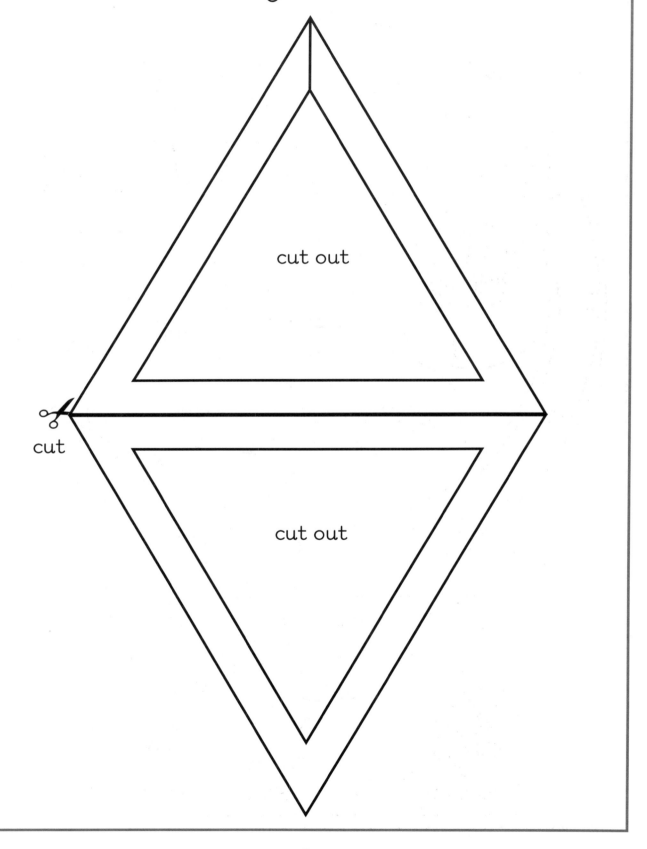

cut out

cut

cut out

How many hats?

◆ Count the hats.

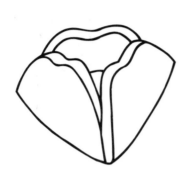

There is

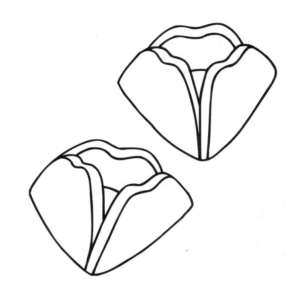

There are

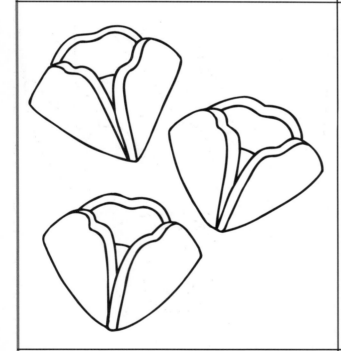

There are

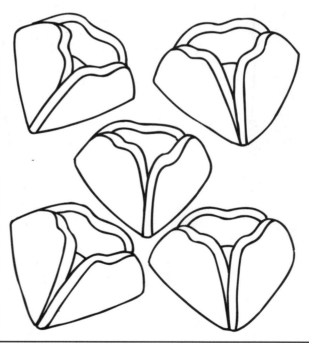

There are

French fish

◆ Match and finish the patterns. Cut out and join.

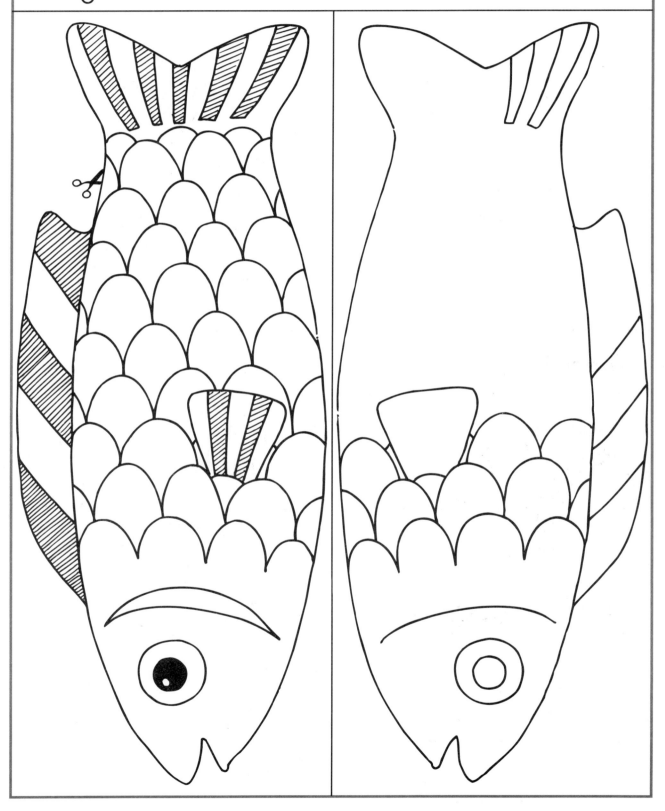

The Khalsa story

◆ Cut out the pictures and put them in order.

Letter links

◆ Match the pictures to the letters.

May parade

◆ Make a banner. Cut the fringe.

cut

Spring flowers

◆ Cut out and make a flower.

roll up to
make stalk

cut along lines

Carp lanterns

◆ Colour the long fish red and the short fish yellow.

Iris hunt

◆ Throw the dice and follow the arrows.

Start

Hidden fish

◆ Find the fish.

SUMMER FESTIVALS

PAGE 37

SHAVUOT – MOSES' LADDER

Learning objective
To count up and down.
(Mathematics)

Group size
Up to four children.

Talk about ladders and how they are used to help people climb up and down to reach high places. Give each child a copy of the photocopiable sheet and a counter. You will need a dice. Explain that you are all going to play a game going up the left ladder. Let the children take turns to throw the dice and move their counters the right number of rungs up the ladder. Ask everyone to count together. The first to the top wins! Repeat, using the second ladder as a number line, subtracting the number on the dice. Encourage all the children to count together.

PAGE 38

SHAVUOT – MOSES ON THE MOUNT

Learning objective
To sequence the story of the ten commandments.
(Language and Literacy)

Group size
Eight children.

Tell the children a version of the story of Moses on the Mount, found in Exodus 31, 32 (Good News Bible). Talk about the story together. Give each

child a copy of the photocopiable sheet and read the sentences together. Can they remember the order of the story? Ask them to cut out the pictures and stick them in the correct sequence of the story.

PAGE 39

DRAGON BOAT FESTIVAL – PADDLE!

Learning objective
To recognize and match colours.
(Creative Development)

Group size
Six children.

Mark a cube sides with red, dark blue, pale blue, yellow, pale green and dark green. Show the children a picture of a colourful dragon boat and talk about the colours they are painted. Talk about the different shades of colour – light and dark – and show the children the cube, naming the colours together. Give each pair of children a copy of the photocopiable sheet and decide which boat each will race. Provide them with the appropriate coloured pencils or pens. Let them throw the dice in turns and colour in the labelled sections correctly. The first completed boat wins!

PAGE 40

DRAGON BOAT FESTIVAL – SINKING FEELING

Learning objective
To investigate floating and sinking objects.
(Knowledge and Understanding of the World)

Group size
Four children.

Provide a small tank or bowl of water and a collection of objects, including a pencil, a stone, a button and a cork. Hold up each object and ask the children to guess whether it will float or sink. Let them take turns to test their ideas. After each try say: 'Why do you think that happened?'. Discuss what materials the objects are made of. Give each child a copy of the photocopiable sheet and invite them to cut out the objects and glue them onto the picture to show whether they floated or sunk.

PAGE 41
DRAGON BOAT FESTIVAL – FLYING FREE

Learning objective
To develop pencil control. (Language and Literacy)

Group size
Eight to ten children.

Show the children some pictures of kites. What colours and shapes can they see? Some are shaped like different creatures. Explain how people who fly kites hold onto the strings of the kites to control them. Give each child a copy of the photocopiable sheet and three different-coloured pencils. Explain that all the owners have tangled their strings. Using a different colour for each kite string, ask them to follow each string very carefully to discover which person flies which kite.

PAGE 42
WESAK – FEARSOME FACES

Learning objective
To make a Buddhist-style festival mask. (Creative Development)

Group size
Six to eight children.

Have a collection of fabric, paper scraps, sequins, beads and shiny foil. Talk about the brightly-coloured masks that Buddhists often use as decorations, these are often fearsome faces to protect them. Give each child a photocopiable sheet copied or mounted onto card and let them cut and glue the scraps and trimmings to make bold masks. When these are dry, cut eye-holes and attach elastic to let the children wear their masks. Make up a dance or form a procession.

PAGE 43
WESAK – LOTUS BLOSSOMS

Learning objective
To make paper lotus blossom offerings. (Knowledge and Understanding of the World)

Group size
Four or five children.

Discuss how people give presents and explain that Buddhists make gifts of lotus blossoms in their temples. Give each child a copy of the photocopiable sheet and a short stick. Provide thick, white and pink paints or colours. Let the children cut out the lotus shape and help them to cut two tiny slits at the 'X' mark in the centre. Suggest that they colour the lotus in white and pink. When dry, push the stick through the slits and tape in place. With the coloured side outwards, bend up the petals into a bud shape and fix them with a dab of glue. Display bunches of the lotuses in vases.

PAGE 44
WESAK – TREE DRESSING

Talk about decorations and lights. Explain that Buddhists often hang pretty lanterns in trees when they celebrate festivals. Give each child a copy of the photocopiable sheet and look at the different trees, counting the branches together. Point out the number boxes and explain that this is the number of lanterns that they have to put in each tree. Let the children colour the lanterns brightly, cut them out and glue the right number onto the branches of each tree.

Learning objective
To match numbers to objects. (Mathematics)

Group size
Eight to ten children.

PAGE 45
WESAK – PRINCE SIDDHATHA

Retell the story of how Prince Siddhatha was born, obtained Enlightenment and passed away (Buddhists do not say died) on the same date many years apart. A good version of this story can be found in *Introducing religions – Buddhism* (Heinemann). Give each child a copy of the photocopiable sheet and talk about the pictures, reading the sentences together. Establish the sequence of events by asking questions such as: 'Did this picture happen before or after this one?'. Let the children cut out the pictures and glue them onto a sheet of paper in the correct story order. Encourage older children to add some speech bubbles and act as a scribe for younger children.

Learning objective
To sequence the main events of Buddha's life. (Knowledge and Understanding of the World).

Group size
Eight children.

PAGE 46
RAKSHA BANDHAN – A GOOD MATCH

Tell the children that Hindu sisters make or buy decorated thread bracelets to give to their brothers. Talk about different sorts of jewellery and decorative designs. Give each child a copy of the photocopiable sheet and ask them to look carefully at the different bracelet patterns. Ask them to try to link the matching pairs with a pencil line.

PAGE 47
RAKSHA BANDHAN – FAMILIES

Talk about families and how these can be very different in size and composition – be sensitive to the possible variations. Ask the children to name the people that they live with and help them to count them. Give each child a copy of the photocopiable sheet and look at the pictures together. Talk about the people in the pictures and decide which is the largest/smallest family. Encourage the children to count the family members in each picture, including the babies, and write the number in the box.

PAGE 48
RAKSHA BANDHAN – HOW TALL?

Talk about people's different heights. Ask the children to stand up and see who is the tallest/shortest. Help them stand in a line with the shortest first, carefully stressing: 'Is she/he taller/shorter than him/her?' to help the children make comparisons (this will need to be dealt with sensitively). Give each child a copy of the photocopiable sheet and a red and blue pencil. Discuss the different pictures. Encourage the children to draw a red circle around the tallest in each group and a blue circle around the shortest. Compare and discuss the results.

PAGE 49
FATHER'S DAY – WASHING LINE

Talk about giving gifts on Father's Day – especially socks! Have a collection of pairs of different-coloured socks. Jumble them up and let the children sort them into pairs. Add them together. Select two pairs of socks and show the children. Count them together and then take one away. Say: 'Four socks take away one sock leaves how many?'. Count them together to check. Repeat with other selections. Now give each child a copy of the photocopiable sheet and ask them to work out how many socks there are on each washing line. Ensure that the children are familiar with the addition and subtraction signs.

PAGE 50
MIDSUMMER'S DAY – SUNNY DAYS

Talk about winter and summer and ask the children to say what differences there are. Ask them whether it is dark or light when they go to bed in the winter and summer. Discuss when

lights are used at home, in streets and cars. Write 'winter' and 'summer' for the children to see. Give each child a copy of the photocopiable sheet and look together at the pictures. Talk about the clues in each one and let them decide whether it is winter or summer, copying the word underneath.

PAGE 51

ST SWITHIN'S DAY – UMBRELLAS!

Learning objective
To develop number recognition and matching skills. (Mathematics)

Group size
Eight to ten children.

Talk about wet weather and what people wear to keep dry. Show the children an umbrella and demonstrate how it works. Look at the different materials it is made of. Give each child a copy of the photocopiable sheet and have a set of coloured pencils available. Explain that each number stands for a colour and show them the key. Let them colour in the names to remind them and then match the numbers and colour the picture.

PAGE 52

ST SWITHIN'S DAY – WATER, WATER!

Learning objective
To learn that bigger containers hold more water. (Mathematics)

Group size
Six to eight children.

Provide different-sized containers, a jug and sticky labels. Fill the containers and ask the children to look closely at the shape and size of each one. Ask them to guess which container holds the most water, and which the least. Tip the contents of each container in turn into the jug, marking the level with a sticky label. Decide together how to order them from 'holds the most' to 'holds the least'. Give each child a copy of the photocopiable sheet and invite them to cut out the pictures and put them in order of how much water they will hold, from most to least.

PAGE 53

O'BAN – LIGHT UP THE FIRE

Talk about the different ways people heat and light their homes and how they cook their food. Show illustrations from history books to show how things were different in the past before electricity and gas. Talk about how people manage when there is no power, for example, when people go camping or during power cuts. Give each child a copy of the photocopiable sheet and ask them to tick the correct title for each picture. Read the words for younger children.

Learning objective
To understand that heating and cooking appliances have changed over time. (Knowledge and Understanding of the World)

Group size
Eight children.

PAGE 54

GARNESH-CHATURTHI – MOVING HOUSE

Talk about the different homes people and animals live in. Show some pictures of people's homes from around the world. Ask the children to describe their own homes. Ask them if anyone has moved house. What did it feel like? Give each child a copy of the photocopiable sheet and ask them to cut out the creatures and stick them to the home that would be best for them. Ask older children to write ' A .... lives in a ....' under each picture.

Learning objective
To understand that different animals live in particular homes. (Knowledge and Understanding of the World)

Group size
Six to eight children.

Moses' ladder

◆ Throw a dice to move up and down the ladders.

up

down

| 10 |
| q |
| 8 |
| 7 |
| 6 |
| 5 |
| 4 |
| 3 |
| 2 |
| 1 |

| 10 |
| q |
| 8 |
| 7 |
| 6 |
| 5 |
| 4 |
| 3 |
| 2 |
| 1 |

Moses on the mount

◆ Cut out the pictures and put them in order.

Moses puts the tablets in a special ark.

Moses hears God's words.

Moses is angry with the people and the tablets break.

Moses goes up the mountain.

Paddle!

◆ Play a game to colour the paddles.

Sinking feeling

◆ Cut out the objects. Stick them above or below the water.

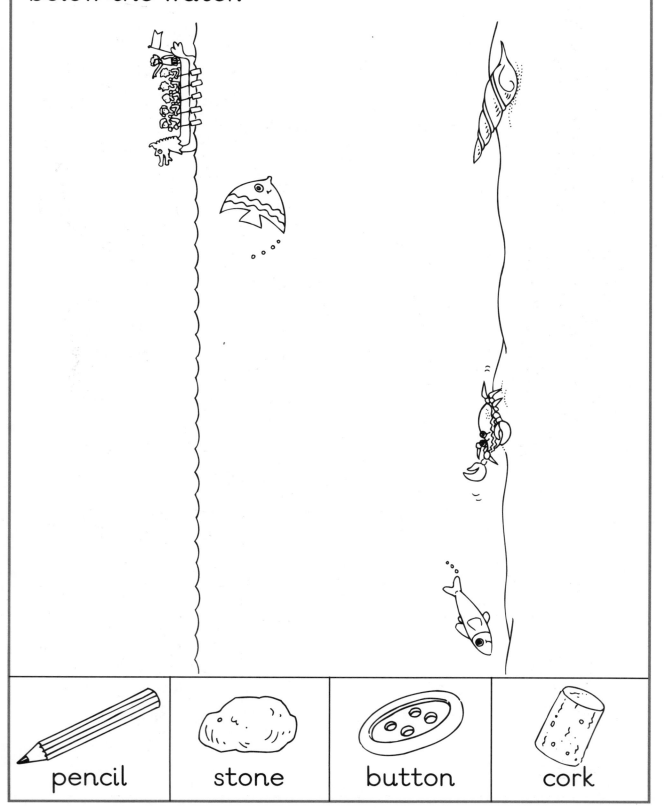

| pencil | stone | button | cork |

Flying free

◆ Use three colours to colour the kite strings.

Fearsome faces

◆ Decorate to make a mask.

Lotus blossoms

◆ Cut and paint to make a lotus flower.

Tree dressing

◆ Cut out the lanterns and hang the right number in the trees.

Prince Siddhatha

◆ Cut out the pictures and put them in order.

Prince Siddhatha discovered the world.

Buddha teaches the people.

Siddhatha under the bodhi tree.

Prince Siddhatha lived in his palace.

A good match

◆ Draw arrows to join the matching bracelets.

Families

◆ Count the people in each family.

How tall?

◆ Draw circles round the biggest and smallest people in each group.

Washing line

◆ Count the socks.

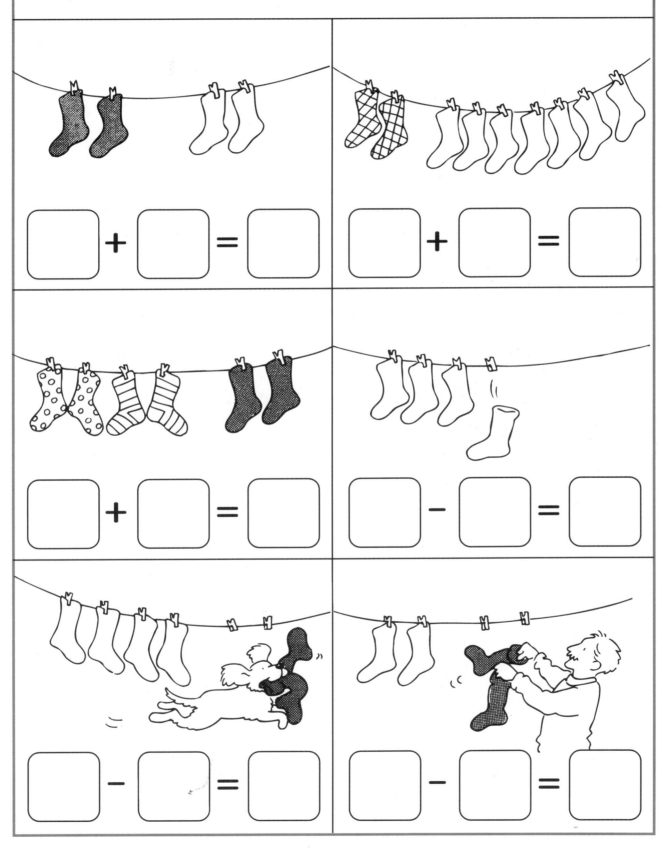

Sunny days

◆ Write the words winter or summer underneath each picture.

Umbrellas!

◆ Use the key to colour the picture.

1 = red
2 = blue
3 = green
4 = yellow
5 = orange
6 = pink
7 = black

Water, water!

◆ Which holds the most water? Put the pictures in order.

Light up the fire

◆ Are the pictures old or new? Tick the right boxes.

old ☐   new ☐

old ☐   new ☐

old ☐   new ☐

old ☐   new ☐

old ☐   new ☐

old ☐   new ☐

Moving house

◆ Match the animal to its home.

AUTUMN FESTIVALS

PAGE 59
CHINESE MOON FESTIVAL – ALL LIT UP!

Learning objective
To match similar lanterns. (Mathematics)

Group size
Eight children.

Ask the children to talk about occasions when they have seen lanterns or special lights, such as for Christmas or outside at barbecue parties and so on. If possible, have a collection of different lanterns and talk about the difference between those lit by electricity and candles, stressing the danger of naked flames. Give each child a copy of the photocopiable sheet and encourage them to look at the different animal shapes. Ask them to link matching pairs with a pencil line. Invite older children to count and write the total number of lanterns.

PAGE 60
CHINESE MOON FESTIVAL – MOON FACES

Learning objective
To make moon puppets. (Knowledge and Understanding of the World)

Group size
Four to six children.

Provide a simple chart of the moon's phases and show the children how the moon shape changes as it goes around the Earth. Explain how the mountains and craters on the moon often make it appear to have a face. Give each child a copy of the photocopiable sheet mounted onto card. Let them cut out the moons and decorate them with gold and black glitter to show the shadow. Fasten them to a plastic straw and encourage them to use them to make up stories to act out.

PAGE 61
ETHIOPIAN NEW YEAR – RASTAFARIAN COLOURS

Learning objective
To make a weaving in Ethiopian national colours. (Creative Development)

Group size
Four children.

Give each child a copy of the photocopiable sheet mounted onto card. Provide a collection of red, green and gold strips of paper, fabric and felt-tipped pens. Let the children colour in each row as labelled. Show the children a piece of loose-weave fabric and pull it apart to show them how the threads are woven under and over the warp. Help the children to cut carefully up the lines and then let them choose the coloured strips to weave through. Seal the ends down carefully to create a woven effect.

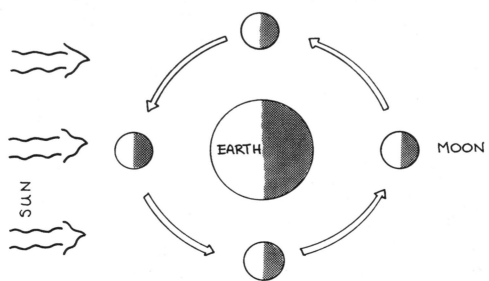

PAGE 62

SUKKOT – SPECIAL HUTS

Learning objective
To make a sukkah. (Physical Development)

Group size
Six children.

Ask the children to think of how natural decorations are often used for special events, such as holly and ivy at Christmas, flowers for weddings and so on. Provide a collection of different leaves and fruits. Explain to the children how Jewish families build a simple sukkah shelter and decorate it with fruit and greenery. Let each child colour in the sukkah and furniture and then cut out and glue on some fruit and leaves from tissue paper and collage materials. Encourage older children to draw different fruits and add them to the beams.

PAGE 63

SUKKOT – LULAV BRANCHES

Learning objective
To construct traditional lulavs. (Knowledge and Understanding of the World)

Group size
Four children.

Explain that at a special synagogue service at Sukkot, Jewish people carry lulavs (mixed shrub branches) and an etrog (lemon) to remind themselves to worship God with all their bodies. The palm stands for the spine, the willow the lips, the myrtle the eyes and the etrog the heart. Give each child a copy of the photocopiable sheet and talk about the different leaf shapes. Count the leaves and fruit, letting older children write the numbers on each leaf. Let them colour the leaves in different greens, cut them out and fasten them together.

PAGE 64

HARVEST – COUNT THE CROP

Learning objective
To count and match apples to trees. (Mathematics)

Group size
Six to eight children.

Provide several pieces of fruit and place them in small groups on the table. Ask the children: 'How many in this group?' 'And in this group?'. Move them together and count them all saying: 'How many altogether?'. Write the numbers beside the groups. Repeat, devising different groups and totals. Then let the children choose different pieces of fruit to make their own addition sums. Give each child a copy of the photocopiable sheet and ask them to count the fruit and write the numbers in the boxes.

PAGE 65

HARVEST – WHERE DOES IT GROW?

Learning objective
To learn that different crops grow above and below the soil. (Knowledge and Understanding of the World)

Group size
Six children.

Pass around different vegetables, one at a time. Ask the children what it looks, feels and smells like. Show the children the roots, stalks and leaves.

Explain that some vegetables grow mostly above the soil and that others grow below, in the dark. Sort the vegetables into 'above the soil' and 'below the soil' groups. Give each child a copy of the photocopiable sheet and ask them to cut out the vegetables and stick them where they would grow – above or below the soil. Let older children draw and add further examples of their own.

PAGE 66

HARVEST – TASTY MATCHES

Learning objective
To match food sources and products. (Knowledge and Understanding of the World)

Group size
Four to six children.

Do the children often go shopping with their families? What sort of food do they usually buy? Now make a list of the food that the children ate for their breakfast or lunch. Explain that some of the foods are grown in the ground or on trees and some come from animals. Cut up the list and sort the foods into 'animal' and 'vegetable' groups. Give each child a copy of the photocopiable sheet and ask them to cut out the pictures. Help them to match the food with the animal or crop that it came from. Explain that some animals or crops produce more than just one type of food.

PAGE 67

HARVEST – NUT HUNT

Learning objective
To find and count hidden nuts. (Mathematics)

Group size
Eight children.

Explain to the children that some animals go to sleep during the cold winter months, but before they do, some of them, such as squirrels, hide some food so that it is there for them when they wake up from their hibernation. Give each child a copy of the photocopiable sheet and tell them that this squirrel has forgotten where he has hidden his nuts. Ask the children to circle each one and write the number beside it. Ask older children to mark some more hiding places and swap sheets with a partner.

PAGE 68

GRANDPARENT'S DAY – NOW AND THEN

Learning objective
To learn that things change over time. (Knowledge and Understanding of the World)

Group size
Six to eight children.

If possible, invite a grandparent to talk to the children about their childhood. Ask them to talk about things that have changed from when they were little. Encourage the children to talk about the differences and similarities in these changes. If possible, look at some old toys together. Give each child a copy of the photocopiable sheet and let them cut out the pictures, gluing them onto a large sheet marked 'Now' and 'Then'.

Invite older children to talk about their decisions.

PAGE 69

DIVALI – HAPPY DAYS

Learning objective
To fold and decorate a Divali card. (Creative Development)

Group size
Four children.

Provide each child with a copy of the photocopiable sheet, some felt-tipped pens, glue and glitter. Talk about greetings cards and how these are sent at special times. Let the children look at the Divali pattern on the sheet and ask them to match and complete the missing section. Encourage them to use bright colours to colour it in. Show them how to fold their sheet like an accordion, providing help as required. Flatten the sheet and add glitter to the background areas. When dry, gently refold and stand up the cards.

PAGE 70

DIVALI – LAMPS

Learning objective
To develop counting and matching skills. (Mathematics)

Group size
Six to eight children.

Explain to the children that during Divali, it is traditional to light lamps. Talk about the different patterns and types of lamp – showing examples if possible. Give each child a copy of the photocopiable sheet and ask them to look carefully at the pictures. Prompt them with questions to encourage them to look closely, such as: 'Count the flames, are they the same?' and 'Count the pattern shapes, are they the same as this one?'. Encourage the children to draw circles round all the differences.

PAGE 71

DIVALI – THE SIXTH GURU

Learning objective
To sequence the story of Guru Hargobind. (Language and Literacy)

Group size
Eight to ten children.

Tell the children the story of Guru Hargobind and his special cloak, a version can be found in *Themes for Early Years – Autumn and Winter Festivals* (Scholastic). Give each child a copy of the photocopiable sheet and a strip of paper measuring 42cm x 14cm. Look at the pictures together and ask the children if the picture shows the beginning, middle or end of the story. Let them cut out and sort the pictures, then glue them to the strip in the correct sequence. Fold the strips to make zigzag books.

PAGE 73

GURU NANAK'S BIRTHDAY – PUZZLE

Provide a collection of objects beginning with c, b, r and p and matching letter labels. Hold up each object and ask what sound it begins with. Sort the objects into labelled groups. Give each child a copy of the photocopiable sheet and yellow, blue, black and brown colours. Look at the turban, asking what sound 'cap' begins with. Explain how to use the key to find the colour that goes with the letter sound. Let the children colour the picture by solving the sound puzzle.

Learning objective
To match initial letter sounds. (Language and Literacy)

Group size
Four to six children.

PAGE 72

BONFIRE NIGHT – WHIZZ BANG!

Learning objective
To make wax-resist pictures. (Creative Development)

Group size
Six to eight children.

Discuss fireworks and the different colours and ways they light up the sky. Ask the children to describe the shapes, colours and noises of the fireworks they know. Stress the safety aspects of enjoying fireworks. Give each child a copy of the photocopiable sheet and a pale-coloured crayon. Ask the children to press quite hard to colour in the fireworks, leaving the background blank. Show them how to wash over their pictures with thin black paint. Explain how the wax 'resists' the paint colouring the paper.

PAGE 74

ST ANDREW'S DAY – SAILING AWAY

Provide a collection of small boats or objects. Put a group of four together and count them. Remove two and say: 'Four take away two leaves how many?'. Repeat with some other numbers. Give each child a copy of the photocopiable sheet and look together at the first picture. Count and say the number sentence together. Encourage the children to count the boats and write the numbers and totals in the boxes. Concentrate on the practical work with younger children, encouraging them to use the correct mathematical language.

Learning objective
To count and subtract fishing boats. (Mathematics)

Group size
Six children.

All lit up!

◆ Match the lanterns.

Moon faces

◆ Cut out and decorate.

Rastafarian colours

◆ Cut along the lines and weave with red, green and gold strips.

red   green   gold   red   green   gold   red   green   gold

Special huts

◆ Decorate the sukkah.

Lulav branches

◆ Colour, cut out and fasten together.

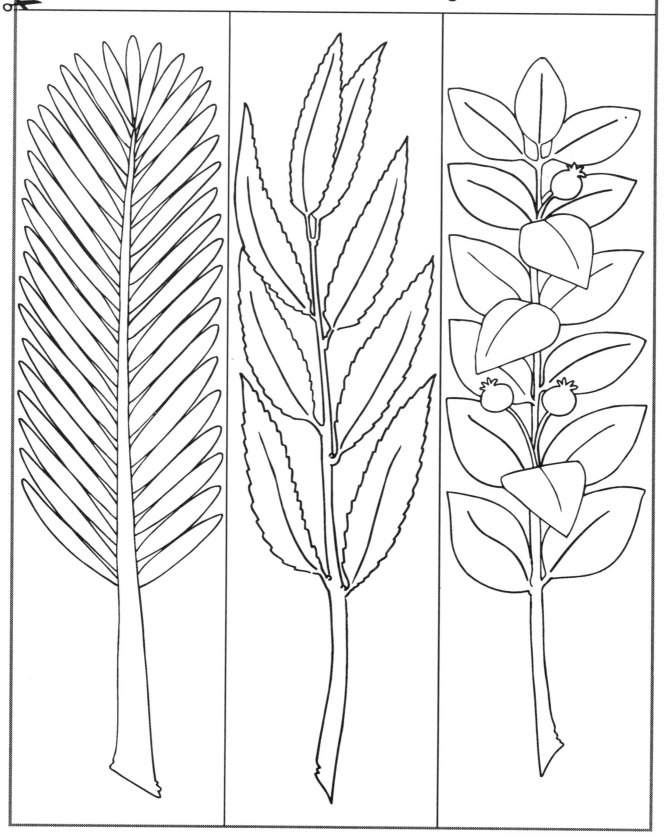

Count the crop

◆ Count the fruit.

How many
apples?

How many
pears?

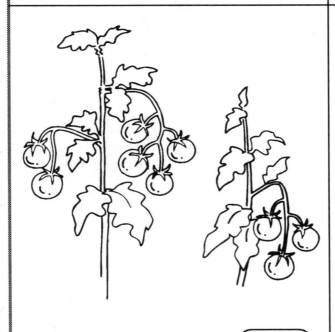

How many
tomatoes?

How many
strawberries?

Where does it grow?

◆ Cut out and stick the food where it grows.

| carrot | cabbage | corn | potatoes | peas | beetroot |

Tasty matches

◆ Cut out and sort the pictures.

Nut hunt

◆ The squirrel has lost ten nuts. Can you find them?

Now and then

✂ ◆ Cut out and sort the pictures.

Happy days

◆ Complete the pattern and decorate.

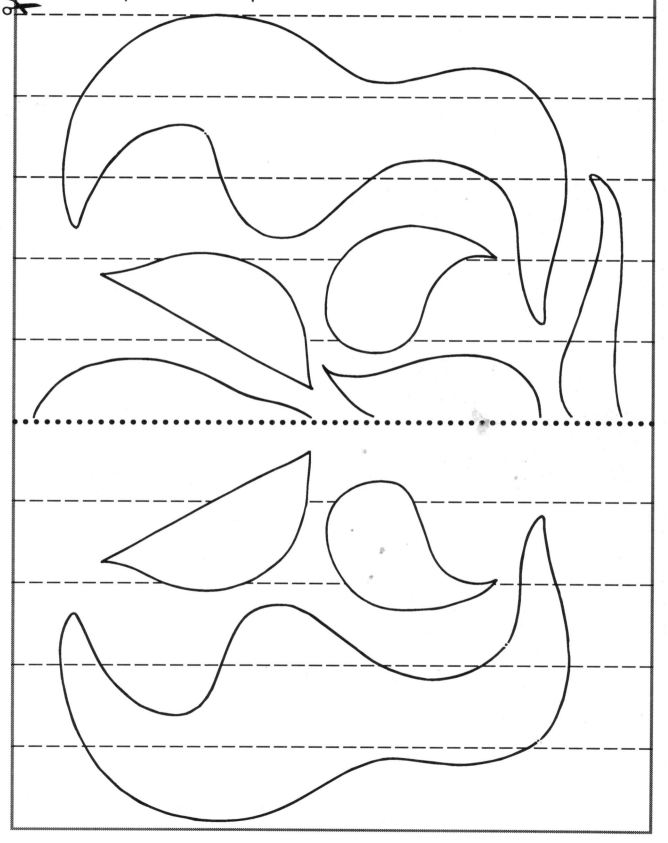

Lamps

◆ Spot the differences.

The sixth Guru

◆ Cut out the pictures and put them in order.

Guru Hargobind is sent to prison.

Everyone can go free.

A special cloak is made.

52 Hindu princes are with him in prison.

Whizz bang!

◆ Colour with a pale crayon and paint black.

Puzzle

◆ Use the key to colour the picture.

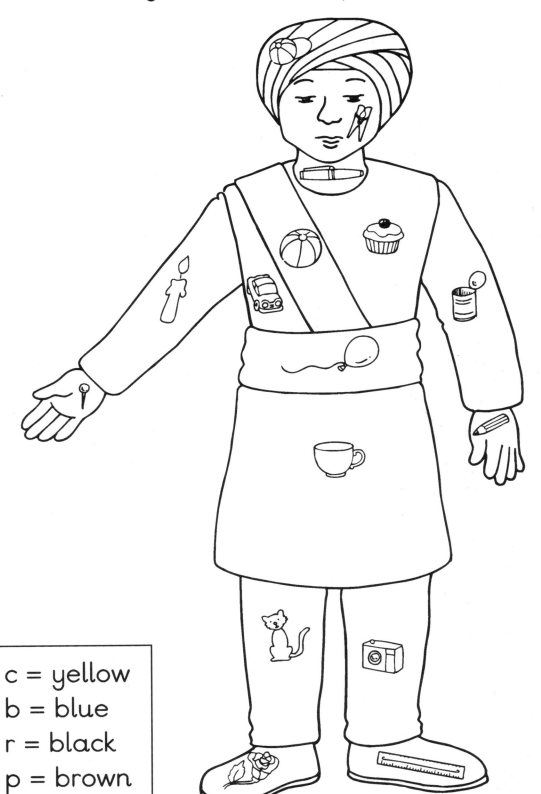

c = yellow
b = blue
r = black
p = brown

Sailing away

◆ Count the boats.

6 − 2 = ☐

4 − 1 = ☐

8 − ☐ = ☐

3 − ☐ = ☐

8 − ☐ = ☐

☐ − ☐ = ☐

WINTER FESTIVALS

PAGE 79
HANUKKAH – CANDLE COUNTING

Provide a collection of candles and labels numbered from 1 to 10. Make a group of five candles, counting them together and labelling them correctly. Repeat several times with different numbers. Then let the children sort the candles into groups and label them correctly. Give each child a copy of the photocopiable sheet and ask them to cut out the candles and stick them onto the hanukiah. Enlarge the sheet for younger children to use.

PAGE 80
HANUKKAH – KIPPAH PATTERNS

Look at some pictures or examples of prayer caps and talk about the patterns and shape of the hats which are made to fit the head. Provide a selection of bright paper scraps and sequins, scissors, glue and sticky tape. Give each child a copy of the photocopiable sheet

and help them to cut out the cap. Let them decorate the kippah attractively. Fold and tape the flap underneath to make the right shape. Ask the children to model their kippahs (using hairgrips) and talk about their chosen patterns and colours.

PAGE 81
CHRISTMAS – DEAR SANTA...

Ask the children about things that they hope they will get given as presents at Christmas time. Have they made a list for Santa yet? Give each child a copy of the photocopiable sheet and read it together. Show the children how the letter begins with the words 'Dear..' and ends with the name of the sender. Talk about the ways the children have been good and help them to write in examples, acting as scribe where needed. Repeat for the present requests, letting younger children draw pictures and older ones write in the words. Make sure parents get a copy!

PAGE 82
CHRISTMAS – TWELVE GIFTS

Teach the children the song 'The Twelve Days of Christmas' (Traditional). Hold up number cards to match the verses as you sing and encourage the children to make suitable actions. Explain that a long time ago, people used to celebrate Christmas from Christmas Day until Twelfth Night. Give each child an enlarged copy of the photocopiable sheet and ask them to cut out the pictures and numbers. Count and sort

them together. Ask individual children to find and match specific numbers, paying attention to any children who are having difficulties.

Ask the children to glue the correct number to the back of the picture. Encourage older children to work unaided.

PAGE 83
CHRISTMAS – SNOW PRINTS

Learning objective
To match footprints to their owners. (Physical Development)

Group size
Eight children.

Discuss winter weather and talk about what happens when it snows. Explain how marks in fresh snow can give us clues as to who has been passing by. Talk about the tracks left by boots, paws and tyres. Give each child a copy of the photocopiable sheet and discuss the tracks together. Ask the children to guess what might have made the tracks. Let the children join the tracks to their owners with a pencil line.

PAGE 84
NEW YEAR – WHAT'S NEW?

Learning objective
To recognize and label old and new objects. (Knowledge and Understanding of the World)

Group size
Six to eight children.

Talk to the children about new things and new beginnings. Provide some pictures of objects of different ages and labels saying 'old' and 'new'. Discuss each object and help the children to decide which group to put it in. Ask them to explain their choices. Give each child a copy of the photocopiable sheet and talk about the pictures, helping them to decide whether to write the word old or new. Ask older children to draw the modern/old equivalent on the reverse side of each picture.

PAGE 85
NEW YEAR – JANUS' FACE

Explain that the Roman God, Janus (from which the word January is derived), had two faces so that he could look in both directions at once. Give each child a copy of the photocopiable sheet. Talk about the things that happened last year and let them draw in their most important events on one side of the page. Act as scribe to help label these. Then let the children draw a picture of something that they think will happen this year on the other side of the page. Let older children write their own words.

Learning objective
To develop imagination. (Language and Literacy)

Group size
Eight children.

PAGE 86
EPIPHANY – SILHOUETTES

Provide a torch and a sheet of card. Ask a child to hold out their hand and shine the torch so that it throws a shadow on the card. Draw round the shadow and compare it to the child's hand. Talk about the similarities. Discuss shadows and when we see them. Give each child a copy of the photocopiable sheet and ask them to study the different kings' shadows. Focus on the differences in the kings' headwear, their gifts and the shape of their cloaks. Ask the children to draw arrows to match the kings with their shadows. Can the children explain their choices?

Learning objective
To match silhouettes to figures. (Knowledge and Understanding of the World)

Group size
Six children.

CHINESE NEW YEAR – LANTERN LIGHTS

PAGE 87

Learning objective
To make paper lanterns. (Physical Development)

Group size
Four children.

Explain to the children that paper lanterns are used as decorations for the Chinese New Year celebrations. Give each child a copy of the photocopiable sheet and let them colour in the shape very brightly. Ask them to cut out the shape and fold it along the marked line. Help them to cut along the lines, starting from the fold and leaving 2cm from the edge uncut. Unfold the paper, leaving a barrel shape, and tape the short sides together. Put thread through the 'X' marks to suspend the lanterns.

CHINESE NEW YEAR – LION DANCE

PAGE 88

Learning objective
To make a simple moving puppet. (Physical Development)

Group size
Four to six children.

Provide a selection of collage materials, glitter, glue, and sticky tape, plus two short sticks, fabric (about 30cm x 20cm) and a copy of the photocopiable sheet, mounted on card for each child. Ask the children to cut out the head and fold it as shown on the sheet. Ask them to decorate their mask very brightly. Help the children to fasten the sticks to the reverse side of the head and jaw and tape the fabric over the lion's back (see diagram above). Now use the sticks to make the puppet dance.

EID-UL-FITR – EID MUBARAK!

PAGE 89

Learning objective
To make a cut-out Eid card. (Creative Development)

Group size
Four children.

Talk to the children about greetings cards and if possible show them an Eid card, explaining that the card is folded from back to front as Arabic is written in this way. Give each child a copy of the photocopiable sheet and ask them to fold the card along the lines. While the card is still folded, help them to cut out the marked sections. Explain that 'Eid Mubarak' is a greeting and ask them to complete the words. Invite them to make the final touches by decorating the mosque and moon.

EID-UL-FITR – FACING EAST

PAGE 90

Learning objectives
To design a prayer mat and learn about compass directions. (Knowledge and Understanding of the World)

Group size
Six children.

Explain to the children that Muslims face east, towards the holy city of Mecca, when they say their prayers. Give each child a copy of the photocopiable sheet and talk about the illustration of the Ka'bah, which Muslims wish to visit at least once in their lifetimes. Let them decorate the prayer mat and help them to cut the 'fringe'. Show the children a compass and explain how people use them to find out the direction they are facing. Display the mats pointing east.

CANDLEMAS – ST MARY'S TEARS

PAGE 91

Learning objective
To sequence the growth cycle of a snowdrop. (Knowledge and Understanding of the World)

Group size
Eight children.

Explain how snowdrops are one of the few winter flowers and how they grow from tiny bulbs. Have a bulb and pictures to show the children. Discuss how bulbs grow with the shoots coming up first and then the roots. Give each child a copy of the photocopiable sheet and ask them to cut the pictures out. Starting with the planting scene, ask the children to put the pictures in the right order.

PANCAKE DAY – FLIP AND RUN!

PAGE 92

Learning objective
To play a counting game. (Mathematics)

Group size
Six to nine children.

Talk to the children about making and tossing pancakes and the local customs of pancake races. If possible, enlarge the photocopiable sheet and provide one between three children. Give each group a dice plus a counter for each child. Let children choose their lane. In turn, ask them to 'flip' the dice, moving their counters along to match

the thrown number. Explain that if they throw a five or a six they have dropped the pancake and they must miss a turn while they pick it up! The first home wins.

PAGE 93

MARDI GRAS – CARNIVAL FUN

Learning objective
To make a carnival mask. (Creative Development)

Group size
Four children.

Provide a selection of collage scraps and trimmings. Talk about masks and why these might be worn for parties. Show the children pictures of butterflies and ask them to look at the colours and patterns. Give each child a copy of the photocopiable sheet mounted on card. Explain that the butterfly's pattern needs completing and ask the children to draw this so that both wings match. Invite them to decorate the mask with bright colours. Help them to cut out the eye holes and attach elastic.

PAGE 94

MARDI GRAS – SOMETHING'S CHANGED

Learning objective
To develop observation and visual discrimination skills. (Language and Literacy)

Group size
Eight children.

Give each child a copy of the photocopiable sheet. Explain that there are ten differences in the two pictures and the children will have to look very carefully to spot them. Take it in turns to see who can find one and describe where it is. Prompt them with questions, such as: 'Tell us where to look. Is it on a person?' 'What are they wearing?' 'What is nearby?'. After all the children have had a turn, invite them to draw circles round all the differences.

PAGE 95

VALENTINE'S DAY – WRAPPING PAPER

Show the children some pieces of wrapping paper that have clear patterns and designs. Ask the children to look at them and describe them. What designs would be suitable for Valentine's Day? Provide some felt-tipped pens and give each child a copy of the photocopiable sheet. Talk about the symbols on the sheet – hearts, flowers and kisses. Why do you think these symbols are on Valentine's Day paper? Draw the children's attention to the way that the rows repeat the pattern down the page. Count the rows and the total number of each symbol together. Let the children draw in the missing symbols and colour the design.

Learning objective
To improve pencil control and make repeating patterns. (Language and Literacy)

Group size
Six to ten children.

PAGE 96

VALENTINE'S DAY – SPECIAL FRIENDS

Talk about friends and what makes them special. Ask the children to talk about the things that their friends do for them that make them feel happy. What things do they like to do together? Explain that everyone can have several friends and that they can like them for different reasons. Give each child a copy of the photocopiable sheet and look at the 'hearts' together. Help them to fill the hearts with the information requested. Act as reader and scribe for younger children. Make a book of all the children's charts, and make sure that all the children have been included.

Learning objective
To complete a special friends chart. (Language and Literacy)

Group size
Three to four children.

Candle counting

◆ Cut out the candles and glue to the
hanukiah.

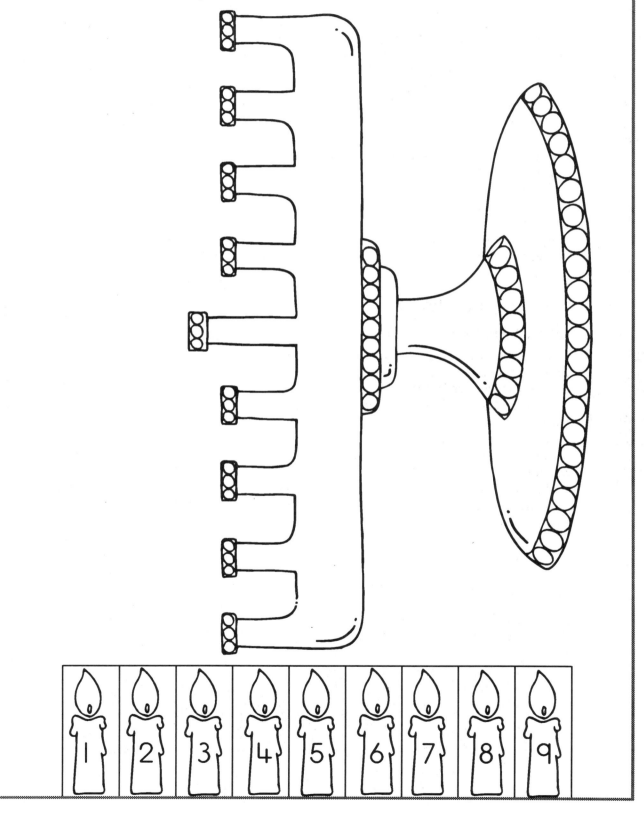

Kippah patterns

◆ Cut out and decorate to make a kippah.

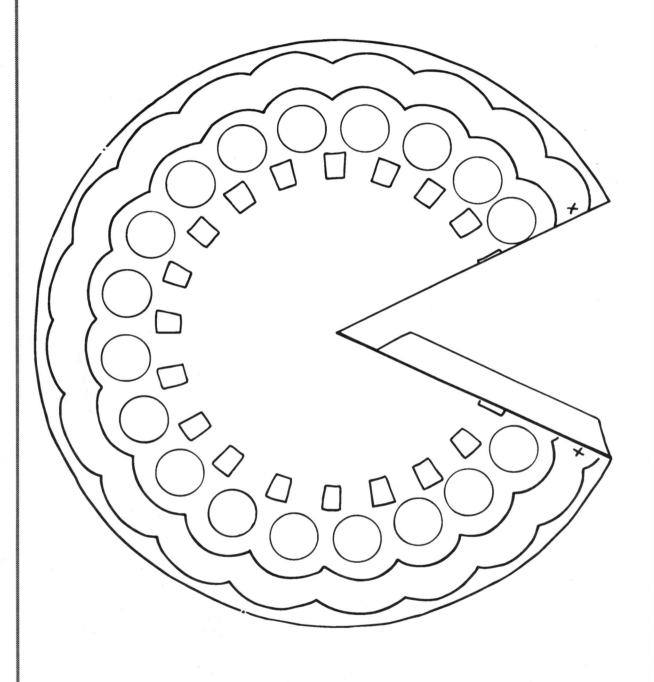

Dear Santa...

◆ Write a letter to Santa.

Dear Santa,
I have been very good. I have...

For Christmas I would like ...

love from

Twelve gifts

◆ Cut out the pictures and numbers and match them together.

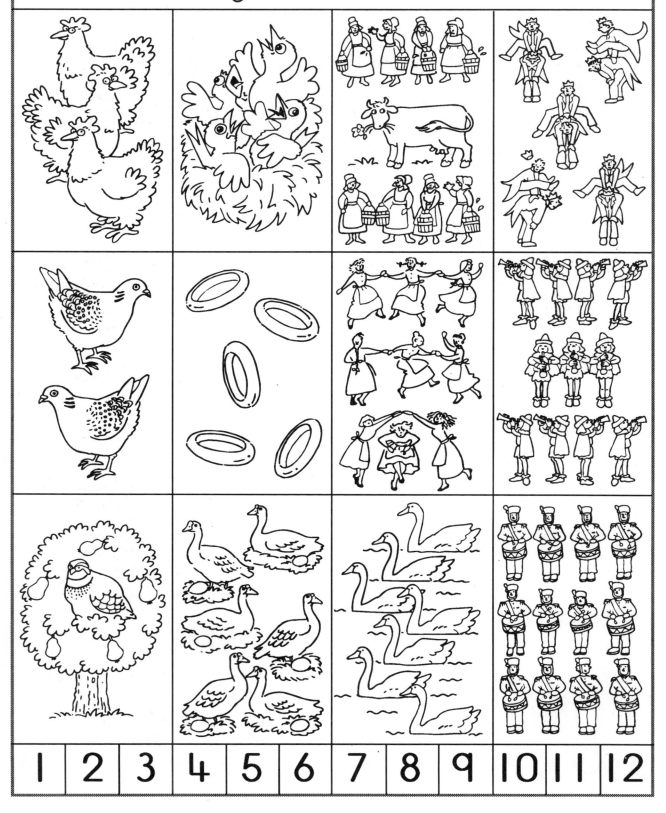

Snow prints

◆ Draw arrows to match the tracks to their owners.

What's new?

◆ Write the word old or new under each picture.

Janus' face

◆ Draw something you did last year and something you want to do this year.

This year

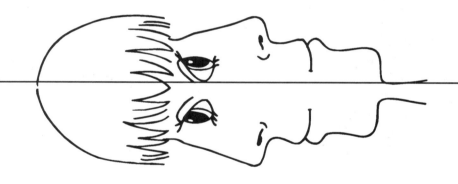

Last year

Silhouettes

◆ Match the kings to their shadows.

Lantern lights

◆ Cut and fold to make a lantern.

fold

Lion dance

◆ Cut out, fold and decorate to make a puppet.

Eid Mubarak!

◆ Make an Eid card.

Facing east

◆ Decorate the prayer mat.

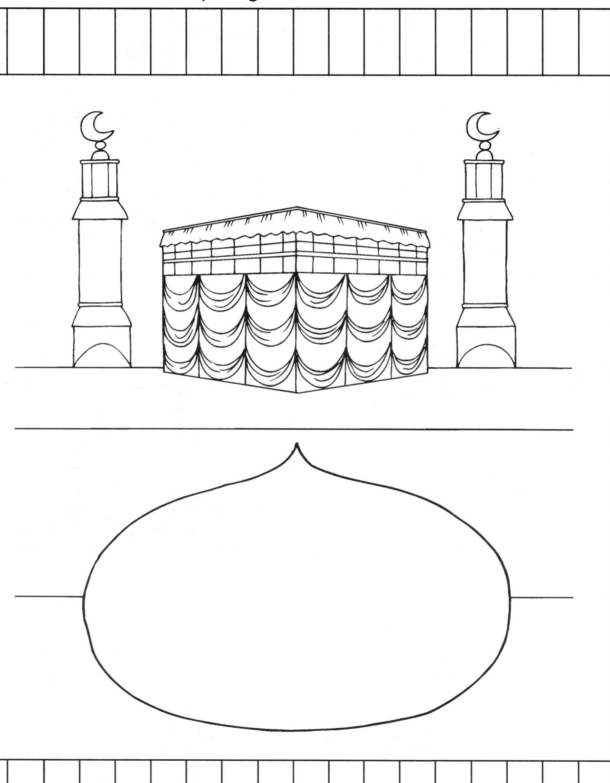

St Mary's tears

◆ Cut out the pictures and put them in order.

Flip and run!

◆ Play the game with two friends.

FINISH

Carnival fun

◆ Match the pattern and make a mask.

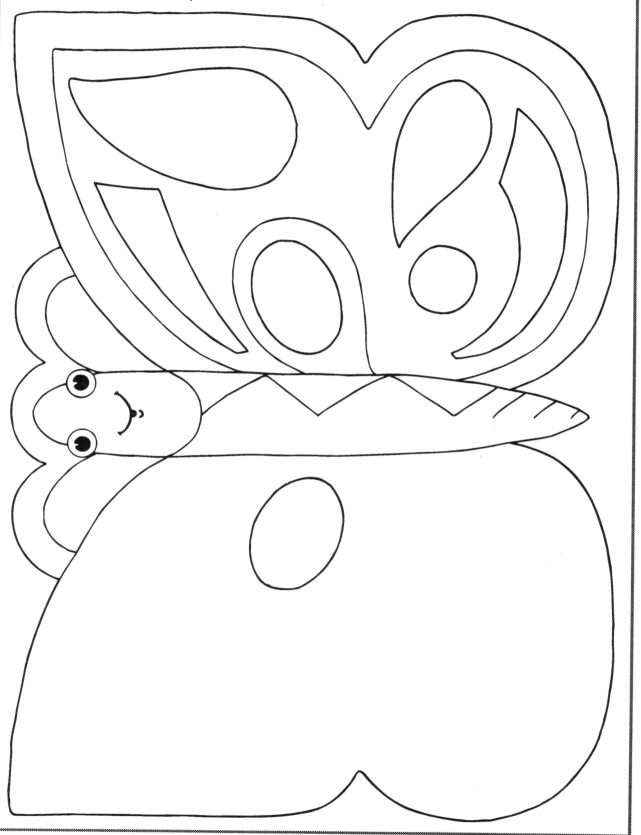

Something's changed

◆ Circle the ten differences.

Wrapping paper

◆ Complete the patterns.

♡	♡	♡	♡
✿	✿	✿	
✕	✕		
♡			
✿			
✕			
♡			
✿			
✕			

Special friends

◆ Write inside the hearts.

My name is...

My friends are...

I like them because...

I like it when we...